FUCK IT

2022

PLANNER FOR SARCASTICALLY GIFTED WOMEN

This belongs to

_____

_____

Contents

Goals & Shit List

2022 Bucket List

Fucket Bucket to make sure you don't waste your precious fucks

Insults & Comebacks for dealing with assholes

2022-2023 Year-at-a-Glance Calendars

Month-at-a-Glance and Weekly/Daily planning calendars with

- Motivational swear quotes and affirmations
- US, UK and CA holidays
- *Important Shit* priority lists
- *Fucking grateful for…* gratitude prompts
- *Notes & Shit* entries

Journal pages for your *Brilliant Thoughts & Shit*

You are fucking amazing

And you need a planner that really gets that. One that's funny, fun to use and will help you get shit done.

Strong women use strong language!
Language that's as creative and colorful as you are and helps you deal with assholes and bullshit.

This planner is filled with motivational swear quotes and affirmations to help you laugh and stay positive as fuck.

You'll also find gratitude prompts and checklists to make sure you're saving your fucks for important shit.

All in a clear, easy-to-use format that will help you stay focused and avoid shitshows.

So drop those fbombs! Let those fucks fly! Be your awesome self!

And enjoy the kickass year you deserve.

Starting. Right. Fucking. Now.

Goals & shit

What goals do you want to crush with your awesomeness? Self care, relationships, hobbies, work? Your possibilities are endless.

_____

_____

_____

_____

_____

_____

_____

_____

_____

_____

_____

_____

_____

_____

_____

_____

_____

_____

_____

_____

_____

2022 Bucket List

What would you fucking love to do this year? Big stuff, small stuff...
it's all good. Write that shit here and check it off when you do it.

_____

_____

_____

_____

_____

_____

_____

_____

_____

_____

_____

_____

_____

_____

_____

_____

_____

_____

_____

_____

Fucket Bucket

Toxic people, negative thoughts and other
shit that won't get your precious fucks.

_____

_____

_____

_____

_____

_____

_____

_____

_____

_____

_____

_____

_____

_____

_____

_____

_____

_____

_____

_____

_____

_____

Insults & Comebacks

Assholes are everywhere. With this handy list of putdowns, you'll never be at a loss for words. There's room to add more favorites.

I'd agree with you but then we'd both be fucking wrong.

Are you always this stupid? Or is today a special occasion?

You make me wish I had more middle fingers.

Why is it acceptable for you to be an asshole but not for me to point it out?

You look like a million I-don't-give-a-fucks.

If you say you don't like me and still watch everything I do… bitch, you're a fan.

I'm jealous of everyone who hasn't met you.

Karma's only a bitch if you are. So brace yourself.

Impressive. You have even more shit coming from your mouth than your ass.

Great news. Size does matter and you are an enormous dick.

If you find me offensive, then I suggest you stop finding me.

Whoever told you to be yourself gave you bad advice.

When I said, "How fucking stupid can you be?"… it wasn't a challenge.

I'm not insulting you. I'm describing you.

You don't have to repeat yourself. I ignored you fine the first time.

Keep rolling your eyes. Maybe you'll find your brain back there.

I just baked you some shut-the-fuckupcakes.

I didn't mean to push your buttons. I was just looking for mute.

You're not as bad as people say. You're MUCH worse.

You're about as useful as a knitted condom.

_____

_____

_____

_____

_____

2022

January

S	M	T	W	T	F	S
						1
2	3	4	5	6	7	8
9	10	11	12	13	14	15
16	17	18	19	20	21	22
23	24	25	26	27	28	29
30	31					

February

S	M	T	W	T	F	S
		1	2	3	4	5
6	7	8	9	10	11	12
13	14	15	16	17	18	19
20	21	22	23	24	25	26
27	28					

March

S	M	T	W	T	F	S
		1	2	3	4	5
6	7	8	9	10	11	12
13	14	15	16	17	18	19
20	21	22	23	24	25	26
27	28	29	30	31		

April

S	M	T	W	T	F	S
					1	2
3	4	5	6	7	8	9
10	11	12	13	14	15	16
17	18	19	20	21	22	23
24	25	26	27	28	29	30

May

S	M	T	W	T	F	S
1	2	3	4	5	6	7
8	9	10	11	12	13	14
15	16	17	18	19	20	21
22	23	24	25	26	27	28
29	30	31				

June

S	M	T	W	T	F	S
			1	2	3	4
5	6	7	8	9	10	11
12	13	14	15	16	17	18
19	20	21	22	23	24	25
26	27	28	29	30		

July

S	M	T	W	T	F	S
					1	2
3	4	5	6	7	8	9
10	11	12	13	14	15	16
17	18	19	20	21	22	23
24	25	26	27	28	29	30
31						

August

S	M	T	W	T	F	S
	1	2	3	4	5	6
7	8	9	10	11	12	13
14	15	16	17	18	19	20
21	22	23	24	25	26	27
28	29	30	31			

September

S	M	T	W	T	F	S
				1	2	3
4	5	6	7	8	9	10
11	12	13	14	15	16	17
18	19	20	21	22	23	24
25	26	27	28	29	30	

October

S	M	T	W	T	F	S
						1
2	3	4	5	6	7	8
9	10	11	12	13	14	15
16	17	18	19	20	21	22
23	24	25	26	27	28	29
30	31					

November

S	M	T	W	T	F	S
		1	2	3	4	5
6	7	8	9	10	11	12
13	14	15	16	17	18	19
20	21	22	23	24	25	26
27	28	29	30			

December

S	M	T	W	T	F	S
				1	2	3
4	5	6	7	8	9	10
11	12	13	14	15	16	17
18	19	20	21	22	23	24
25	26	27	28	29	30	31

2023

January

S	M	T	W	T	F	S
1	2	3	4	5	6	7
8	9	10	11	12	13	14
15	16	17	18	19	20	21
22	23	24	25	26	27	28
29	30	31				

February

S	M	T	W	T	F	S
			1	2	3	4
5	6	7	8	9	10	11
12	13	14	15	16	17	18
19	20	21	22	23	24	25
26	27	28				

March

S	M	T	W	T	F	S
			1	2	3	4
5	6	7	8	9	10	11
12	13	14	15	16	17	18
19	20	21	22	23	24	25
26	27	28	29	30	31	

April

S	M	T	W	T	F	S
						1
2	3	4	5	6	7	8
9	10	11	12	13	14	15
16	17	18	19	20	21	22
23	24	25	26	27	28	29
30						

May

S	M	T	W	T	F	S
	1	2	3	4	5	6
7	8	9	10	11	12	13
14	15	16	17	18	19	20
21	22	23	24	25	26	27
28	29	30	31			

June

S	M	T	W	T	F	S
				1	2	3
4	5	6	7	8	9	10
11	12	13	14	15	16	17
18	19	20	21	22	23	24
25	26	27	28	29	30	

July

S	M	T	W	T	F	S
						1
2	3	4	5	6	7	8
9	10	11	12	13	14	15
16	17	18	19	20	21	22
23	24	25	26	27	28	29
30	31					

August

S	M	T	W	T	F	S
		1	2	3	4	5
6	7	8	9	10	11	12
13	14	15	16	17	18	19
20	21	22	23	24	25	26
27	28	29	30	31		

September

S	M	T	W	T	F	S
					1	2
3	4	5	6	7	8	9
10	11	12	13	14	15	16
17	18	19	20	21	22	23
24	25	26	27	28	29	30

October

S	M	T	W	T	F	S
1	2	3	4	5	6	7
8	9	10	11	12	13	14
15	16	17	18	19	20	21
22	23	24	25	26	27	28
29	30	31				

November

S	M	T	W	T	F	S
			1	2	3	4
5	6	7	8	9	10	11
12	13	14	15	16	17	18
19	20	21	22	23	24	25
26	27	28	29	30		

December

S	M	T	W	T	F	S
					1	2
3	4	5	6	7	8	9
10	11	12	13	14	15	16
17	18	19	20	21	22	23
24	25	26	27	28	29	30
31						

December 2021-January 2022

27 MONDAY	28 TUESDAY	29 WEDNESDAY
_____	_____	_____
_____	_____	_____
_____	_____	_____
_____	_____	_____
_____	_____	_____
_____	_____	_____
_____	_____	_____
_____	_____	_____
_____	_____	_____
_____	_____	_____
_____	_____	_____
○ _____	○ _____	○ _____
○ _____	○ _____	○ _____
○ _____	○ _____	○ _____
○ _____	○ _____	○ _____
○ _____	○ _____	○ _____
○ _____	○ _____	○ _____
○ _____	○ _____	○ _____
○ _____	○ _____	○ _____
○ _____	○ _____	○ _____

Important as *fuck*

Fucking grateful for...

Out with the old shit. In with the new awesome.

30 THURSDAY

_____
_____
_____
_____
_____
_____
_____
_____
_____
_____
_____
_____

- ○ _____
- ○ _____
- ○ _____
- ○ _____
- ○ _____
- ○ _____
- ○ _____
- ○ _____
- ○ _____

31 FRIDAY

_____
_____
_____
_____
_____
_____
_____
_____
_____
_____
_____

- ○ _____
- ○ _____
- ○ _____
- ○ _____
- ○ _____
- ○ _____
- ○ _____
- ○ _____
- ○ _____

1 SATURDAY
New Year's Day

_____
_____
_____
_____
- ○ _____
- ○ _____
- ○ _____

2 SUNDAY

_____
_____
_____
_____
- ○ _____
- ○ _____
- ○ _____

Notes and shit

_____
_____
_____

JANUARY 2022

Sunday	Monday	Tuesday	Wednesday
2	3	4	5
9	10	11	12
16	17 Martin Luther King Jr. Day (US)	18	19
23	24	25	26
30	31		

Make 2022 your bitch

Thursday	Friday	Saturday	Important shit
		1 New Year's Day	
6	7	8	
13	14	15	
20	21	22	
27	28	29	

December 2021

S	M	T	W	T	F	S
			1	2	3	4
5	6	7	8	9	10	11
12	13	14	15	16	17	18
19	20	21	22	23	24	25
26	27	28	29	30	31	

February 2022

S	M	T	W	T	F	S
		1	2	3	4	5
6	7	8	9	10	11	12
13	14	15	16	17	18	19
20	21	22	23	24	25	26
27	28					

January 2022

	3 MONDAY	4 TUESDAY	5 WEDNESDAY

○ _____
○ _____
○ _____
○ _____
○ _____
○ _____
○ _____
○ _____
○ _____

Important as *fuck*

_____
_____
_____

Fucking grateful for...

_____
_____
_____

Inhale the good shit. Exhale the bullshit.

6 THURSDAY

_____
_____
_____
_____
_____
_____
_____
_____
_____
_____
_____

○ _____
○ _____
○ _____
○ _____
○ _____
○ _____
○ _____
○ _____
○ _____

7 FRIDAY

_____
_____
_____
_____
_____
_____
_____
_____
_____
_____

○ _____
○ _____
○ _____
○ _____
○ _____
○ _____
○ _____
○ _____
○ _____

8 SATURDAY

_____
_____
_____
_____
○ _____
○ _____
○ _____

9 SUNDAY

_____
_____
_____
_____
_____
○ _____
○ _____
○ _____

Notes and shit

_____
_____
_____

January 2022

10 MONDAY   11 TUESDAY   12 WEDNESDAY

Important as *fuck*

Fucking grateful for...

Keep your head high and your middle finger higher

13 THURSDAY

_____
_____
_____
_____
_____
_____
_____
_____
_____
_____
_____

○ _____
○ _____
○ _____
○ _____
○ _____
○ _____
○ _____
○ _____
○ _____

14 FRIDAY

_____
_____
_____
_____
_____
_____
_____
_____
_____

○ _____
○ _____
○ _____
○ _____
○ _____
○ _____
○ _____
○ _____
○ _____

15 SATURDAY

_____
_____
_____
_____
_____
○ _____
○ _____
○ _____

16 SUNDAY

_____
_____
_____
_____
_____
○ _____
○ _____
○ _____

Notes and shit

_____
_____
_____

January 2022

17 MONDAY
Martin Luther King Jr. Day (US)

18 TUESDAY

19 WEDNESDAY

Important as fuck

Fucking grateful for...

Do more of what makes you fucking happy

20 THURSDAY

_____
_____
_____
_____
_____
_____
_____
_____
_____
_____
_____
- ○ _____
- ○ _____
- ○ _____
- ○ _____
- ○ _____
- ○ _____
- ○ _____
- ○ _____
- ○ _____

21 FRIDAY

_____
_____
_____
_____
_____
_____
_____
- ○ _____
- ○ _____
- ○ _____
- ○ _____
- ○ _____
- ○ _____
- ○ _____
- ○ _____
- ○ _____

22 SATURDAY

_____
_____
_____
_____
- ○ _____
- ○ _____
- ○ _____

23 SUNDAY

_____
_____
_____
_____
_____
- ○ _____
- ○ _____
- ○ _____

Notes and shit

_____
_____
_____

January 2022

You are a fucking unicorn.

24 MONDAY	25 TUESDAY	26 WEDNESDAY

Important as fuck

_____

_____

_____

Fucking grateful for...

_____

_____

_____

Just resist the urge to stab assholes with your head.

27 THURSDAY

_____
_____
_____
_____
_____
_____
_____
_____
_____
_____
_____

- ◯ _____
- ◯ _____
- ◯ _____
- ◯ _____
- ◯ _____
- ◯ _____
- ◯ _____
- ◯ _____
- ◯ _____

28 FRIDAY

_____
_____
_____
_____
_____
_____
_____
_____
_____
_____

- ◯ _____
- ◯ _____
- ◯ _____
- ◯ _____
- ◯ _____
- ◯ _____
- ◯ _____
- ◯ _____
- ◯ _____

29 SATURDAY

_____
_____
_____
_____
_____

- ◯ _____
- ◯ _____
- ◯ _____

30 SUNDAY

_____
_____
_____
_____

- ◯ _____
- ◯ _____
- ◯ _____

Notes and _shit_

_____
_____
_____

FEBRUARY 2022

Sunday	Monday	Tuesday	Wednesday
		1	2
6	7	8	9
13	14 Valentine's Day	15	16
20	21 President's Day (US)	22	23
27	28		

Fuck perfect

Thursday	Friday	Saturday	Important shit
3	4	5	
10	11	12	
17	18	19	
24	25	26	

January

S	M	T	W	T	F	S
						1
2	3	4	5	6	7	8
9	10	11	12	13	14	15
16	17	18	19	20	21	22
23	24	25	26	27	28	29
30	31					

March

S	M	T	W	T	F	S
		1	2	3	4	5
6	7	8	9	10	11	12
13	14	15	16	17	18	19
20	21	22	23	24	25	26
27	28	29	30	31		

January-February 2022

31 MONDAY	1 TUESDAY	2 WEDNESDAY

Important as fuck

Fucking _grateful for..._

Be kind as fuck to yourself

3 THURSDAY   **4 FRIDAY**   **5 SATURDAY**

_____   _____   _____
_____   _____   _____
_____   _____   _____
_____   _____   _____
_____   _____   _____
_____   _____   _____
_____   _____   ○ _____
_____   _____   ○ _____
_____   _____   ○ _____
_____   _____

6 SUNDAY

_____   _____   _____
○ _____   ○ _____   _____
○ _____   ○ _____   _____
○ _____   ○ _____   _____
○ _____   ○ _____   _____
○ _____   ○ _____
○ _____   ○ _____
○ _____   ○ _____   ○ _____
○ _____   ○ _____   ○ _____
○ _____   ○ _____   ○ _____

Notes and shit

_____
_____
_____

February 2022

7 MONDAY	8 TUESDAY	9 WEDNESDAY
_____	_____	_____
_____	_____	_____
_____	_____	_____
_____	_____	_____
_____	_____	_____
_____	_____	_____
_____	_____	_____
_____	_____	_____
_____	_____	_____
_____	_____	_____
_____	_____	_____
_____	_____	_____
○ _____	○ _____	○ _____
○ _____	○ _____	○ _____
○ _____	○ _____	○ _____
○ _____	○ _____	○ _____
○ _____	○ _____	○ _____
○ _____	○ _____	○ _____
○ _____	○ _____	○ _____
○ _____	○ _____	○ _____
○ _____	○ _____	○ _____

Important as *fuck*

Fucking grateful for...

Your inner critic is a total bitch. Ignore her.

10 THURSDAY

_____
_____
_____
_____
_____
_____
_____
_____
_____
_____
_____

- ⭕ _____
- ⭕ _____
- ⭕ _____
- ⭕ _____
- ⭕ _____
- ⭕ _____
- ⭕ _____
- ⭕ _____
- ⭕ _____

11 FRIDAY

_____
_____
_____
_____
_____
_____
_____
_____
_____
_____

- ⭕ _____
- ⭕ _____
- ⭕ _____
- ⭕ _____
- ⭕ _____
- ⭕ _____
- ⭕ _____
- ⭕ _____
- ⭕ _____

12 SATURDAY

_____
_____
_____
_____

- ⭕ _____
- ⭕ _____
- ⭕ _____

13 SUNDAY

_____
_____
_____
_____
_____
_____

- ⭕ _____
- ⭕ _____
- ⭕ _____

Notes and shit

_____
_____
_____

February 2022

Be yourself. . .

14 MONDAY
Valentine's Day

15 TUESDAY

16 WEDNESDAY

_____
_____
_____
_____
_____
_____
_____
_____
_____
_____
_____

- ◯ _____
- ◯ _____
- ◯ _____
- ◯ _____
- ◯ _____
- ◯ _____
- ◯ _____
- ◯ _____
- ◯ _____

Important as *fuck*

_____
_____
_____

Fucking grateful for...

_____
_____
_____

People don't have to like it and you don't have to give a fuck

17 THURSDAY

_____
_____
_____
_____
_____
_____
_____
_____
_____
_____
_____
_____
_____

- ○ _____
- ○ _____
- ○ _____
- ○ _____
- ○ _____
- ○ _____
- ○ _____
- ○ _____
- ○ _____

18 FRIDAY

_____
_____
_____
_____
_____
_____
_____
_____

- ○ _____
- ○ _____
- ○ _____
- ○ _____
- ○ _____
- ○ _____
- ○ _____
- ○ _____
- ○ _____

19 SATURDAY

_____
_____
_____
_____

- ○ _____
- ○ _____
- ○ _____

20 SUNDAY

_____
_____
_____
_____
_____
_____

- ○ _____
- ○ _____
- ○ _____

Notes and shit

_____
_____
_____

February 2022

21 MONDAY	22 TUESDAY	23 WEDNESDAY
President's Day (US)		

Important as fuck

Fucking grateful for...

A grateful heart is a magnet for more good shit

24 THURSDAY

_____
_____
_____
_____
_____
_____
_____
_____
_____
_____

○ _____
○ _____
○ _____
○ _____
○ _____
○ _____
○ _____
○ _____
○ _____

25 FRIDAY

_____
_____
_____
_____
_____
_____

○ _____
○ _____
○ _____
○ _____
○ _____
○ _____
○ _____
○ _____
○ _____

26 SATURDAY

_____
_____
_____
_____
○ _____
○ _____
○ _____

27 SUNDAY

_____
_____
_____
_____
_____
○ _____
○ _____
○ _____

Notes and shit

_____
_____
_____

MARCH 2022

Sunday	Monday	Tuesday	Wednesday
		1	2
6	7	8 International Women's Day	9
13	14	15	16
20	21	22	23
27 Mother's Day (UK)	28	29	30

Love the fuck out of yourself

Thursday	Friday	Saturday	Important shit
3	4	5	
10	11	12	
17 St. Patrick's Day	18	19	
24	25	26	
31			

February

S	M	T	W	T	F	S
		1	2	3	4	5
6	7	8	9	10	11	12
13	14	15	16	17	18	19
20	21	22	23	24	25	26
27	28					

April

S	M	T	W	T	F	S
					1	2
3	4	5	6	7	8	9
10	11	12	13	14	15	16
17	18	19	20	21	22	23
24	25	26	27	28	29	30

February-March 2022

28 MONDAY	1 TUESDAY	2 WEDNESDAY

Important as *fuck*

Fucking grateful for...

May your bucket list be as long as your fuck-it list

3 THURSDAY

_____
_____
_____
_____
_____
_____
_____
_____
_____
_____
_____

○ _____
○ _____
○ _____
○ _____
○ _____
○ _____
○ _____
○ _____
○ _____

4 FRIDAY

_____
_____
_____
_____
_____
_____
_____
_____
_____
_____

○ _____
○ _____
○ _____
○ _____
○ _____
○ _____
○ _____
○ _____
○ _____

5 SATURDAY

_____
_____
_____
_____
_____
_____

○ _____
○ _____
○ _____

6 SUNDAY

_____
_____
_____
_____
_____

○ _____
○ _____
○ _____

Notes and shit

_____
_____
_____

March 2022

7 MONDAY

_____
_____
_____
_____
_____
_____
_____
_____
_____
_____
_____
_____

○ _____
○ _____
○ _____
○ _____
○ _____
○ _____
○ _____
○ _____
○ _____

8 TUESDAY
International Women's Day

_____
_____
_____
_____
_____
_____
_____
_____
_____
_____
_____
_____

○ _____
○ _____
○ _____
○ _____
○ _____
○ _____
○ _____
○ _____
○ _____

9 WEDNESDAY

_____
_____
_____
_____
_____
_____
_____
_____
_____
_____
_____
_____

○ _____
○ _____
○ _____
○ _____
○ _____
○ _____
○ _____
○ _____
○ _____

Important as *fuck*

_____
_____
_____

Fucking grateful for...

_____
_____
_____

The first five days after the weekend are the hardest

10 THURSDAY

_____
_____
_____
_____
_____
_____
_____
_____
_____
_____
_____
- ○ _____
- ○ _____
- ○ _____
- ○ _____
- ○ _____
- ○ _____
- ○ _____
- ○ _____
- ○ _____

11 FRIDAY

_____
_____
_____
_____
_____
_____
_____
_____
_____
_____
- ○ _____
- ○ _____
- ○ _____
- ○ _____
- ○ _____
- ○ _____
- ○ _____
- ○ _____
- ○ _____

12 SATURDAY

_____
_____
_____
_____
_____
- ○ _____
- ○ _____
- ○ _____

13 SUNDAY

_____
_____
_____
_____
- ○ _____
- ○ _____
- ○ _____

Notes and _shit_

_____
_____
_____

March 2022

The journey of a thousand miles. . .

14 MONDAY	15 TUESDAY	16 WEDNESDAY

Important as fuck

_____
_____
_____

Fucking grateful for...

_____
_____
_____

begins with a single fucking step

17 THURSDAY
St. Patrick's Day

18 FRIDAY

19 SATURDAY

- ○
- ○
- ○

20 SUNDAY

Day 17 (Thursday) tasks
- ○
- ○
- ○
- ○
- ○
- ○
- ○
- ○
- ○

Day 18 (Friday) tasks
- ○
- ○
- ○
- ○
- ○
- ○
- ○
- ○
- ○

Day 20 (Sunday) tasks
- ○
- ○
- ○

Notes and *shit*

March 2022

21 MONDAY	22 TUESDAY	23 WEDNESDAY

_____
_____
_____
_____
_____
_____
_____
_____
_____
_____
_____
_____

○ _____
○ _____
○ _____
○ _____
○ _____
○ _____
○ _____
○ _____
○ _____

Important as *fuck*

_____
_____
_____

Fucking grateful for...

_____
_____
_____

If you can't say something nice, write that shit down

24 THURSDAY

_____
_____
_____
_____
_____
_____
_____
_____
_____
_____
_____

- ○ _____
- ○ _____
- ○ _____
- ○ _____
- ○ _____
- ○ _____
- ○ _____
- ○ _____
- ○ _____

25 FRIDAY

_____
_____
_____
_____
_____
_____
_____
_____
_____

- ○ _____
- ○ _____
- ○ _____
- ○ _____
- ○ _____
- ○ _____
- ○ _____
- ○ _____
- ○ _____

26 SATURDAY

_____
_____
_____
_____
_____

- ○ _____
- ○ _____
- ○ _____

27 SUNDAY
Mother's Day (UK)

_____
_____
_____
_____
_____

- ○ _____
- ○ _____
- ○ _____

Notes and shit

_____
_____
_____

March-April 2022

28 MONDAY	29 TUESDAY	30 WEDNESDAY

Important as *fuck*

Fucking grateful for...

You are a ray of fucking sunshine

31 THURSDAY

_____
_____
_____
_____
_____
_____
_____
_____
_____
_____
_____

- ◯ _____
- ◯ _____
- ◯ _____
- ◯ _____
- ◯ _____
- ◯ _____
- ◯ _____
- ◯ _____
- ◯ _____

1 FRIDAY
April Fools' Day

_____
_____
_____
_____
_____
_____
_____
_____
_____
_____
_____

- ◯ _____
- ◯ _____
- ◯ _____
- ◯ _____
- ◯ _____
- ◯ _____
- ◯ _____
- ◯ _____
- ◯ _____

2 SATURDAY
Ramadan begins at sundown

- ◯ _____
- ◯ _____
- ◯ _____

3 SUNDAY

_____
_____
_____
_____

- ◯ _____
- ◯ _____
- ◯ _____

Notes and shit

_____
_____
_____

APRIL 2022

Sunday	Monday	Tuesday	Wednesday

March

S	M	T	W	T	F	S
		1	2	3	4	5
6	7	8	9	10	11	12
13	14	15	16	17	18	19
20	21	22	23	24	25	26
27	28	29	30	31		

May

S	M	T	W	T	F	S
1	2	3	4	5	6	7
8	9	10	11	12	13	14
15	16	17	18	19	20	21
22	23	24	25	26	27	28
29	30	31				

Sunday	Monday	Tuesday	Wednesday
3	4	5	6
10	11	12	13
17 — Easter	18 — Easter Monday (CA)	19	20
24	25	26	27

Bloom bitch

Thursday	Friday	Saturday	Important shit
	1 April Fools' Day	2 Ramadan begins at sundown	
7	8	9	
14	15 Good Friday Passover, starts at sundown	16	
21	22 Earth Day	23	
28	29	30	

April 2022

Important as *fuck*

Fucking grateful for...

It's a beautiful day to get shit done

7 THURSDAY	8 FRIDAY	9 SATURDAY

_____ _____ _____

_____ _____ _____

_____ _____ _____

_____ _____ _____

_____ _____ _____

_____ _____ _____

_____ _____ ○ _____

_____ _____ ○ _____

_____ _____ ○ _____

_____ _____

10 SUNDAY

_____ _____ _____

○ _____ ○ _____ _____

○ _____ ○ _____ _____

○ _____ ○ _____ _____

○ _____ ○ _____ _____

○ _____ ○ _____ _____

○ _____ ○ _____ ○ _____

○ _____ ○ _____ ○ _____

○ _____ ○ _____ ○ _____

○ _____ ○ _____

Notes and _shit_

_____

_____

_____

Every day may not be a good day...

11 MONDAY   12 TUESDAY   13 WEDNESDAY

Important as *fuck*

Fucking grateful for...

but there's some good shit in every day.

14 THURSDAY

_____
_____
_____
_____
_____
_____
_____
_____
_____
_____
_____

○ _____
○ _____
○ _____
○ _____
○ _____
○ _____
○ _____
○ _____
○ _____

15 FRIDAY
Good Friday, Passover, begins at Sunset

_____
_____
_____
_____
_____
_____
_____
_____
_____
_____
_____

○ _____
○ _____
○ _____
○ _____
○ _____
○ _____
○ _____
○ _____
○ _____

16 SATURDAY

_____
_____
_____
_____
_____

○ _____
○ _____
○ _____

17 SUNDAY
Easter

_____
_____
_____
_____
_____

○ _____
○ _____
○ _____

Notes and shit

_____
_____
_____

April 2022

Important as *fuck*

Fucking grateful for...

You're not a bitch. You're a teller of unfortunate truths.

21 THURSDAY

_____
_____
_____
_____
_____
_____
_____
_____
_____
_____

- ◯
- ◯
- ◯
- ◯
- ◯
- ◯
- ◯
- ◯
- ◯

22 FRIDAY
Earth Day

_____
_____
_____
_____
_____
_____
_____
_____
_____

- ◯
- ◯
- ◯
- ◯
- ◯
- ◯
- ◯
- ◯
- ◯

23 SATURDAY

_____
_____
_____
_____

- ◯
- ◯
- ◯

24 SUNDAY

_____
_____
_____
_____

- ◯
- ◯
- ◯

Notes and shit

_____
_____
_____

April-May 2022

25 MONDAY	26 TUESDAY	27 WEDNESDAY

Important as *fuck*

Fucking grateful for...

Life's too short to hang out with assholes

28 THURSDAY | **29 FRIDAY** | **30 SATURDAY**

_____
_____
_____
_____
_____
_____
_____
_____
_____
_____

- ◯
- ◯
- ◯
- ◯
- ◯
- ◯
- ◯
- ◯
- ◯

_____
_____
_____
_____
_____
_____
_____
_____
_____

- ◯
- ◯
- ◯
- ◯
- ◯
- ◯
- ◯
- ◯
- ◯

_____
_____
_____
_____
_____

- ◯
- ◯
- ◯

1 SUNDAY
Labour Day (UK)

_____
_____

- ◯
- ◯
- ◯

Notes and shit

_____
_____
_____

MAY 2022

Sunday	Monday	Tuesday	Wednesday
1 Labour Day (UK)	2 Early May Bank Holiday (UK)	3	4
8 Mother's Day (US, CA)	9	10	11
15	16	17	18
22	23	24	25
29	30 Memorial Day (US)	31	

Let that shit go

Thursday	Friday	Saturday	Important *shit*
5 Cinco de Mayo (US)	6	7	_____
			_____
12	13	14	_____
			_____
19	20	21 Armed Forces Day (US)	_____
			_____
26	27	28	_____

April

S	M	T	W	T	F	S
					1	2
3	4	5	6	7	8	9
10	11	12	13	14	15	16
17	18	19	20	21	22	23
24	25	26	27	28	29	30

June

S	M	T	W	T	F	S
			1	2	3	4
5	6	7	8	9	10	11
12	13	14	15	16	17	18
19	20	21	22	23	24	25
26	27	28	29	30		

May 2022

2 MONDAY
Early May Bank Holiday (UK)

_____
_____
_____
_____
_____
_____
_____
_____
_____
_____
_____
_____
_____

○ _____
○ _____
○ _____
○ _____
○ _____
○ _____
○ _____
○ _____
○ _____

3 TUESDAY

_____
_____
_____
_____
_____
_____
_____
_____
_____
_____
_____
_____
_____

○ _____
○ _____
○ _____
○ _____
○ _____
○ _____
○ _____
○ _____
○ _____

4 WEDNESDAY

_____
_____
_____
_____
_____
_____
_____
_____
_____
_____
_____
_____
_____

○ _____
○ _____
○ _____
○ _____
○ _____
○ _____
○ _____
○ _____
○ _____

Important as *fuck*

_____
_____
_____

Fucking grateful for...

_____
_____
_____

Feel the fear and do that shit anyway

5 THURSDAY

_____
_____
_____
_____
_____
_____
_____
_____
_____
_____
_____

- ○ _____
- ○ _____
- ○ _____
- ○ _____
- ○ _____
- ○ _____
- ○ _____
- ○ _____
- ○ _____

6 FRIDAY

_____
_____
_____
_____
_____
_____
_____
_____
_____
_____

- ○ _____
- ○ _____
- ○ _____
- ○ _____
- ○ _____
- ○ _____
- ○ _____
- ○ _____
- ○ _____

7 SATURDAY

_____
_____
_____
_____
_____

- ○ _____
- ○ _____
- ○ _____

8 SUNDAY

Mother's Day (US, CA)

_____
_____
_____
_____

- ○ _____
- ○ _____
- ○ _____

Notes and shit

_____
_____
_____

May 2022

In a world where you can be anything, be kind. . .

9 MONDAY	10 TUESDAY	11 WEDNESDAY
_____	_____	_____
_____	_____	_____
_____	_____	_____
_____	_____	_____
_____	_____	_____
_____	_____	_____
_____	_____	_____
_____	_____	_____
_____	_____	_____
_____	_____	_____
_____	_____	_____
○ _____	○ _____	○ _____
○ _____	○ _____	○ _____
○ _____	○ _____	○ _____
○ _____	○ _____	○ _____
○ _____	○ _____	○ _____
○ _____	○ _____	○ _____
○ _____	○ _____	○ _____
○ _____	○ _____	○ _____
○ _____	○ _____	○ _____

Important as fuck

_____

_____

_____

Fucking grateful for...

_____

_____

_____

and kinda bitchy. You're only human after all.

12 THURSDAY

_____
_____
_____
_____
_____
_____
_____
_____
_____
_____

- ○ _____
- ○ _____
- ○ _____
- ○ _____
- ○ _____
- ○ _____
- ○ _____
- ○ _____
- ○ _____

13 FRIDAY

_____
_____
_____
_____
_____
_____
_____

- ○ _____
- ○ _____
- ○ _____
- ○ _____
- ○ _____
- ○ _____
- ○ _____
- ○ _____
- ○ _____

14 SATURDAY

_____
_____
_____
_____
_____

- ○ _____
- ○ _____
- ○ _____

15 SUNDAY

_____
_____
_____
_____
_____

- ○ _____
- ○ _____
- ○ _____

Notes and *shit*

_____
_____
_____

May 2022

16 MONDAY	17 TUESDAY	18 WEDNESDAY

Important as *fuck*

Fucking grateful for...

Tell negative thoughts to fuck off

19 THURSDAY

20 FRIDAY

21 SATURDAY
Armed Forces Day (US)

_____
_____
_____
_____
_____
_____
_____

○ _____
○ _____
○ _____

22 SUNDAY

○ _____   ○ _____
○ _____   ○ _____
○ _____   ○ _____
○ _____   ○ _____
○ _____   ○ _____
○ _____   ○ _____
○ _____   ○ _____   ○ _____
○ _____   ○ _____   ○ _____
○ _____   ○ _____   ○ _____

Notes and *shit*

_____
_____
_____

May 2022

23 MONDAY	24 TUESDAY	25 WEDNESDAY

Important as fuck

Fucking *grateful for...*

You are bullshit proof

26 THURSDAY

_____
_____
_____
_____
_____
_____
_____
_____
_____
_____
_____

○ _____
○ _____
○ _____
○ _____
○ _____
○ _____
○ _____
○ _____
○ _____

27 FRIDAY

_____
_____
_____
_____
_____
_____
_____
_____
_____
_____

○ _____
○ _____
○ _____
○ _____
○ _____
○ _____
○ _____
○ _____
○ _____

28 SATURDAY

_____
_____
_____
_____
_____

○ _____
○ _____
○ _____

29 SUNDAY

_____
_____
_____
_____
_____

○ _____
○ _____
○ _____

Notes and shit

_____
_____
_____

JUNE 2022

Sunday	Monday	Tuesday	Wednesday
			1
5	6	7	8
12	13	14 Flag Day (US)	15
19 Father's Day Juneteenth (US)	20	21	22
26	27	28	29

Aim for progress, not fucking perfection

Thursday	Friday	Saturday	Important shit
2 Spring Bank Holiday (UK)	**3** Queen's Platinum Jubilee (UK)	**4**	
9	**10**	**11**	
16	**17**	**18**	
23	**24**	**25**	
30			

May

S	M	T	W	T	F	S
1	2	3	4	5	6	7
8	9	10	11	12	13	14
15	16	17	18	19	20	21
22	23	24	25	26	27	28
29	30	31				

July

S	M	T	W	T	F	S
					1	2
3	4	5	6	7	8	9
10	11	12	13	14	15	16
17	18	19	20	21	22	23
24	25	26	27	28	29	30
31						

May-June 2022

| 30 MONDAY | 31 TUESDAY | 1 WEDNESDAY |
| Memorial Day (US) | | |

Important as *fuck*

Fucking grateful for...

Do epic shit. And, yes, epic naps count.

2 THURSDAY
Spring Bank Holiday (UK)

3 FRIDAY
Queen's Platinum Jubilee (UK)

4 SATURDAY

○
○
○

5 SUNDAY

2 THURSDAY list
○
○
○
○
○
○
○
○
○

3 FRIDAY list
○
○
○
○
○
○
○
○
○

5 SUNDAY list
○
○
○

Notes and shit

June 2022

6 MONDAY	7 TUESDAY	8 WEDNESDAY
_____	_____	_____
_____	_____	_____
_____	_____	_____
_____	_____	_____
_____	_____	_____
_____	_____	_____
_____	_____	_____
_____	_____	_____
_____	_____	_____
_____	_____	_____
_____	_____	_____
_____	_____	_____
○ _____	○ _____	○ _____
○ _____	○ _____	○ _____
○ _____	○ _____	○ _____
○ _____	○ _____	○ _____
○ _____	○ _____	○ _____
○ _____	○ _____	○ _____
○ _____	○ _____	○ _____
○ _____	○ _____	○ _____
○ _____	○ _____	○ _____

Important as *fuck*

_____

_____

_____

Fucking grateful for...

_____

_____

_____

Have a fucktastic day

9 THURSDAY

_____
_____
_____
_____
_____
_____
_____
_____
_____
_____
_____

○ _____
○ _____
○ _____
○ _____
○ _____
○ _____
○ _____
○ _____
○ _____

10 FRIDAY

_____
_____
_____
_____
_____
_____
_____
_____
_____

○ _____
○ _____
○ _____
○ _____
○ _____
○ _____
○ _____
○ _____
○ _____

11 SATURDAY

_____
_____
_____
_____
_____
○ _____
○ _____
○ _____

12 SUNDAY

_____
_____
_____
_____
○ _____
○ _____
○ _____

Notes and shit

_____
_____
_____

June 2022

13 MONDAY

14 TUESDAY
Flag Day (US)

15 WEDNESDAY

Important as _fuck_

Fucking _grateful for..._

You are fucking beautiful. . . inside and out

16 THURSDAY

17 FRIDAY

18 SATURDAY

○
○
○

19 SUNDAY
Father's Day, Juneteenth (US)

○
○
○
○
○
○
○
○
○

○
○
○
○
○
○
○
○
○

○
○
○

Notes and *shit*

June 2022

20 MONDAY	21 TUESDAY	22 WEDNESDAY

Important as *fuck*

Fucking grateful for...

Save your fucks for important shit

23 THURSDAY

_____
_____
_____
_____
_____
_____
_____
_____
_____
_____
_____
- ○ _____
- ○ _____
- ○ _____
- ○ _____
- ○ _____
- ○ _____
- ○ _____
- ○ _____
- ○ _____

24 FRIDAY

_____
_____
_____
_____
_____
_____
_____
_____
_____
_____
- ○ _____
- ○ _____
- ○ _____
- ○ _____
- ○ _____
- ○ _____
- ○ _____
- ○ _____
- ○ _____

25 SATURDAY

_____
_____
_____
_____
_____
- ○ _____
- ○ _____
- ○ _____

26 SUNDAY

_____
_____
_____
_____
- ○ _____
- ○ _____
- ○ _____

Notes and shit

_____
_____
_____

JULY 2022

Sunday	Monday	Tuesday	Wednesday
3	4 Independence Day (US)	5	6
10	11	12	13
17	18	19	20
24	25	26	27
31			

Manifest that shit

Thursday	Friday	Saturday	Important *shit*
	1 Canada Day (CA)	2	_____ _____ _____ _____
7	8	9	_____ _____ _____ _____ _____
14	15	16	_____ _____ _____ _____
21	22	23	_____ _____ _____ _____
28	29	30	_____ _____ _____ _____

June

S	M	T	W	T	F	S
			1	2	3	4
5	6	7	8	9	10	11
12	13	14	15	16	17	18
19	20	21	22	23	24	25
26	27	28	29	30		

August

S	M	T	W	T	F	S
	1	2	3	4	5	6
7	8	9	10	11	12	13
14	15	16	17	18	19	20
21	22	23	24	25	26	27
28	29	30	31			

June-July 2022

27 MONDAY	28 TUESDAY	29 WEDNESDAY
_____	_____	_____
_____	_____	_____
_____	_____	_____
_____	_____	_____
_____	_____	_____
_____	_____	_____
_____	_____	_____
_____	_____	_____
_____	_____	_____
_____	_____	_____
_____	_____	_____
○ _____	○ _____	○ _____
○ _____	○ _____	○ _____
○ _____	○ _____	○ _____
○ _____	○ _____	○ _____
○ _____	○ _____	○ _____
○ _____	○ _____	○ _____
○ _____	○ _____	○ _____
○ _____	○ _____	○ _____
○ _____	○ _____	○ _____

Important as *fuck*

Fucking grateful for...

Your hobbies include having no time for this shit

30 THURSDAY

_____
_____
_____
_____
_____
_____
_____
_____
_____
_____
○ _____
○ _____
○ _____
○ _____
○ _____
○ _____
○ _____
○ _____
○ _____

1 FRIDAY
Canada Day (CA)

_____
_____
_____
_____
_____
_____
_____
_____
_____
_____
○ _____
○ _____
○ _____
○ _____
○ _____
○ _____
○ _____
○ _____
○ _____

2 SATURDAY

_____
_____
_____
_____
_____
○ _____
○ _____
○ _____

3 SUNDAY

_____
_____
_____
_____
_____
○ _____
○ _____
○ _____

Notes and shit

_____
_____
_____

July 2022

4 MONDAY
Independence Day (US)

5 TUESDAY

6 WEDNESDAY

Important as *fuck*

Fucking grateful for...

Thank you for being fucking awesome

7 THURSDAY	8 FRIDAY	9 SATURDAY

_____
_____
_____
_____
_____
_____
_____
_____
_____
_____
_____

○ _____
○ _____
○ _____
○ _____
○ _____
○ _____
○ _____
○ _____
○ _____

○ _____
○ _____
○ _____
○ _____
○ _____
○ _____
○ _____
○ _____
○ _____

○ _____
○ _____
○ _____

10 SUNDAY

_____
_____
_____
_____
_____

○ _____
○ _____
○ _____

Notes and shit

_____
_____
_____

July 2022

Important as *fuck*

Fucking grateful for...

You're not bossy. You just have better ideas.

14 THURSDAY

_____
_____
_____
_____
_____
_____
_____
_____
_____
_____
_____
_____

- ○ _____
- ○ _____
- ○ _____
- ○ _____
- ○ _____
- ○ _____
- ○ _____
- ○ _____
- ○ _____

15 FRIDAY

_____
_____
_____
_____
_____
_____
_____
_____
_____
_____
_____

- ○ _____
- ○ _____
- ○ _____
- ○ _____
- ○ _____
- ○ _____
- ○ _____
- ○ _____
- ○ _____

16 SATURDAY

_____
_____
_____
_____
_____

- ○ _____
- ○ _____
- ○ _____

17 SUNDAY

_____
_____
_____
_____
_____

- ○ _____
- ○ _____
- ○ _____

Notes and _shit_

_____
_____
_____

July 2022

18 MONDAY	19 TUESDAY	20 WEDNESDAY

Important as *fuck*

Fucking grateful for...

Reminder: No one has all their shit together

21 THURSDAY

_____
_____
_____
_____
_____
_____
_____
_____
_____
_____
_____
_____
_____

- ○ _____
- ○ _____
- ○ _____
- ○ _____
- ○ _____
- ○ _____
- ○ _____
- ○ _____
- ○ _____

22 FRIDAY

_____
_____
_____
_____
_____
_____
_____
_____
_____
_____
_____

- ○ _____
- ○ _____
- ○ _____
- ○ _____
- ○ _____
- ○ _____
- ○ _____
- ○ _____
- ○ _____

23 SATURDAY

_____
_____
_____
_____
_____
- ○ _____
- ○ _____
- ○ _____

24 SUNDAY

_____
_____
_____
_____
_____
- ○ _____
- ○ _____
- ○ _____

Notes and shit

_____
_____
_____

July 2022

25 MONDAY	26 TUESDAY	27 WEDNESDAY

Important as *fuck*

Fucking grateful for...

Thinking is not one of their strengths.

28 THURSDAY

_____
_____
_____
_____
_____
_____
_____
_____
_____
_____
_____

○ _____
○ _____
○ _____
○ _____
○ _____
○ _____
○ _____
○ _____
○ _____

29 FRIDAY

_____
_____
_____
_____
_____
_____
_____
_____

○ _____
○ _____
○ _____
○ _____
○ _____
○ _____
○ _____
○ _____
○ _____

30 SATURDAY

_____
_____
_____

○ _____
○ _____
○ _____

31 SUNDAY

_____
_____
_____
_____
_____

○ _____
○ _____
○ _____

Notes and shit

_____
_____
_____

AUGUST 2022

Sunday	Monday	Tuesday	Wednesday
	1	2	3
7	8	9	10
14	15	16	17
21	22	23	24
28	29 Summer Bank Holiday (UK)	30	31

Wake up. Kick ass. Repeat.

Thursday	Friday	Saturday	Important shit
4	5	6	
11	12	13	
18	19	20	
25	26	27	

July

S	M	T	W	T	F	S
					1	2
3	4	5	6	7	8	9
10	11	12	13	14	15	16
17	18	19	20	21	22	23
24	25	26	27	28	29	30
31						

September

S	M	T	W	T	F	S
				1	2	3
4	5	6	7	8	9	10
11	12	13	14	15	16	17
18	19	20	21	22	23	24
25	26	27	28	29	30	

August 2022

Sarcasm...

1 MONDAY	2 TUESDAY	3 WEDNESDAY
_____	_____	_____
_____	_____	_____
_____	_____	_____
_____	_____	_____
_____	_____	_____
_____	_____	_____
_____	_____	_____
_____	_____	_____
_____	_____	_____
_____	_____	_____
_____	_____	_____
_____	_____	_____
○ _____	○ _____	○ _____
○ _____	○ _____	○ _____
○ _____	○ _____	○ _____
○ _____	○ _____	○ _____
○ _____	○ _____	○ _____
○ _____	○ _____	○ _____
○ _____	○ _____	○ _____
○ _____	○ _____	○ _____
○ _____	○ _____	○ _____

Important as *fuck*

_____
_____
_____

Fucking grateful for...

_____
_____
_____

because slapping the shit out of people is frowned upon

4 THURSDAY

_____
_____
_____
_____
_____
_____
_____
_____
_____
_____
_____

- ○ _____
- ○ _____
- ○ _____
- ○ _____
- ○ _____
- ○ _____
- ○ _____
- ○ _____
- ○ _____

5 FRIDAY

_____
_____
_____
_____
_____
_____
_____
_____
_____
_____

- ○ _____
- ○ _____
- ○ _____
- ○ _____
- ○ _____
- ○ _____
- ○ _____
- ○ _____
- ○ _____

6 SATURDAY

_____
_____
_____
_____

- ○ _____
- ○ _____
- ○ _____

7 SUNDAY

_____
_____
_____
_____
_____

- ○ _____
- ○ _____
- ○ _____

Notes and shit

_____
_____
_____

August 2022

8 MONDAY	9 TUESDAY	10 WEDNESDAY
_____	_____	_____
_____	_____	_____
_____	_____	_____
_____	_____	_____
_____	_____	_____
_____	_____	_____
_____	_____	_____
_____	_____	_____
_____	_____	_____
_____	_____	_____
_____	_____	_____
_____	_____	_____

- ○ _____
- ○ _____
- ○ _____
- ○ _____
- ○ _____
- ○ _____
- ○ _____
- ○ _____
- ○ _____

Important as fuck

_____
_____
_____

Fucking grateful for...

_____
_____
_____

Rise and fucking shine

11 THURSDAY

_____
_____
_____
_____
_____
_____
_____
_____
_____
_____
_____

- ◯ _____
- ◯ _____
- ◯ _____
- ◯ _____
- ◯ _____
- ◯ _____
- ◯ _____
- ◯ _____
- ◯ _____

12 FRIDAY

_____
_____
_____
_____
_____
_____
_____

- ◯ _____
- ◯ _____
- ◯ _____
- ◯ _____
- ◯ _____
- ◯ _____
- ◯ _____
- ◯ _____
- ◯ _____

13 SATURDAY

_____
_____
_____
_____

- ◯ _____
- ◯ _____
- ◯ _____

14 SUNDAY

_____
_____
_____
_____
_____

- ◯ _____
- ◯ _____
- ◯ _____

Notes and shit

_____
_____
_____

August 2022

Kindness is like a boomerang...

15 MONDAY	16 TUESDAY	17 WEDNESDAY

Important as fuck

Fucking grateful for...

Throw that shit around and it will come back to you

18 THURSDAY

_____
_____
_____
_____
_____
_____
_____
_____
_____
_____
_____

- ○ _____
- ○ _____
- ○ _____
- ○ _____
- ○ _____
- ○ _____
- ○ _____
- ○ _____
- ○ _____

19 FRIDAY

_____
_____
_____
_____
_____
_____
_____
_____
_____

- ○ _____
- ○ _____
- ○ _____
- ○ _____
- ○ _____
- ○ _____
- ○ _____
- ○ _____
- ○ _____

20 SATURDAY

_____
_____
_____
_____
_____

- ○ _____
- ○ _____
- ○ _____

21 SUNDAY

_____
_____
_____
_____
_____

- ○ _____
- ○ _____
- ○ _____

Notes and shit

_____
_____
_____

August 2022

Don't compare your real life...

22 MONDAY	23 TUESDAY	24 WEDNESDAY

Important as *fuck*

Fucking grateful for...

To someone else's fake ass highlight reel

25 THURSDAY

_____
_____
_____
_____
_____
_____
_____
_____
_____
_____
_____
_____

○ _____
○ _____
○ _____
○ _____
○ _____
○ _____
○ _____
○ _____
○ _____

26 FRIDAY

_____
_____
_____
_____
_____
_____
_____
_____
_____
_____
_____

○ _____
○ _____
○ _____
○ _____
○ _____
○ _____
○ _____
○ _____
○ _____

27 SATURDAY

_____
_____
_____
_____
_____
○ _____
○ _____
○ _____

28 SUNDAY

_____
_____
_____
_____
_____
_____
○ _____
○ _____
○ _____

Notes and _shit_

_____
_____
_____

SEPTEMBER 2022

Sunday	Monday	Tuesday	Wednesday
August S M T W T F S 　 1 2 3 4 5 6 7 8 9 10 11 12 13 14 15 16 17 18 19 20 21 22 23 24 25 26 27 28 29 30 31	October S M T W T F S 　 　 　 　 　 　 1 2 3 4 5 6 7 8 9 10 11 12 13 14 15 16 17 18 19 20 21 22 23 24 25 26 27 28 29 30 31		
4	5　Labor Day (US, CA)	6	7
11	12	13	14
18	19	20	21
25	26	27	28

You. Can. Do. This. Shit.

Thursday	Friday	Saturday	Important *shit*
1	2	3	
8	9	10	
15	16	17	
22	23	24	
29	30		

August-September 2022

29 MONDAY	30 TUESDAY	31 WEDNESDAY
Summer Bank Holiday (UK)		

29 MONDAY
Summer Bank Holiday (UK)

30 TUESDAY

31 WEDNESDAY

_____

Important as *fuck*

_____

Fucking grateful for...

Look at you kicking ass and shit

1 THURSDAY

_____
_____
_____
_____
_____
_____
_____
_____
_____
_____
_____

○ _____
○ _____
○ _____
○ _____
○ _____
○ _____
○ _____
○ _____
○ _____

2 FRIDAY

_____
_____
_____
_____
_____
_____
_____
_____
_____

○ _____
○ _____
○ _____
○ _____
○ _____
○ _____
○ _____
○ _____
○ _____

3 SATURDAY

_____
_____
_____
_____
○ _____
○ _____
○ _____

4 SUNDAY

_____
_____
_____
_____
_____
○ _____
○ _____
○ _____

Notes and shit

_____
_____
_____

September 2022

If assholes are trying to drag you down. . .

5 MONDAY
Labor Day (US, CA)

_____
_____
_____
_____
_____
_____
_____
_____
_____
_____

- ⚪ _____
- ⚪ _____
- ⚪ _____
- ⚪ _____
- ⚪ _____
- ⚪ _____
- ⚪ _____
- ⚪ _____
- ⚪ _____

6 TUESDAY

_____
_____
_____
_____
_____
_____
_____
_____
_____
_____

- ⚪ _____
- ⚪ _____
- ⚪ _____
- ⚪ _____
- ⚪ _____
- ⚪ _____
- ⚪ _____
- ⚪ _____
- ⚪ _____

7 WEDNESDAY

_____
_____
_____
_____
_____
_____
_____
_____
_____
_____

- ⚪ _____
- ⚪ _____
- ⚪ _____
- ⚪ _____
- ⚪ _____
- ⚪ _____
- ⚪ _____
- ⚪ _____
- ⚪ _____

Important as *fuck*

_____
_____
_____

Fucking grateful for...

_____
_____
_____

it just means you're above them

8 THURSDAY

_____
_____
_____
_____
_____
_____
_____
_____
_____
_____
_____
- ○ _____
- ○ _____
- ○ _____
- ○ _____
- ○ _____
- ○ _____
- ○ _____
- ○ _____
- ○ _____

9 FRIDAY

_____
_____
_____
_____
_____
_____
_____
_____
_____
_____
- ○ _____
- ○ _____
- ○ _____
- ○ _____
- ○ _____
- ○ _____
- ○ _____
- ○ _____
- ○ _____

10 SATURDAY

_____
_____
_____
_____
_____
- ○ _____
- ○ _____
- ○ _____

11 SUNDAY

_____
_____
_____
_____
_____
- ○ _____
- ○ _____
- ○ _____

Notes and shit

_____
_____
_____

September 2022

12 MONDAY	13 TUESDAY	14 WEDNESDAY
_____	_____	_____
_____	_____	_____
_____	_____	_____
_____	_____	_____
_____	_____	_____
_____	_____	_____
_____	_____	_____
_____	_____	_____
_____	_____	_____
_____	_____	_____
_____	_____	_____
_____	_____	_____
_____	_____	_____

○ _____   ○ _____   ○ _____

○ _____   ○ _____   ○ _____

○ _____   ○ _____   ○ _____

○ _____   ○ _____   ○ _____

○ _____   ○ _____   ○ _____

○ _____   ○ _____   ○ _____

○ _____   ○ _____   ○ _____

○ _____   ○ _____   ○ _____

○ _____   ○ _____   ○ _____

Important as *fuck*

_____

_____

_____

Fucking grateful for...

_____

_____

_____

Be bold. Be brave. Be your badass self.

15 THURSDAY

_____
_____
_____
_____
_____
_____
_____
_____
_____
_____
_____

- ○ _____
- ○ _____
- ○ _____
- ○ _____
- ○ _____
- ○ _____
- ○ _____
- ○ _____
- ○ _____

16 FRIDAY

_____
_____
_____
_____
_____
_____
_____

- ○ _____
- ○ _____
- ○ _____
- ○ _____
- ○ _____
- ○ _____
- ○ _____
- ○ _____
- ○ _____

17 SATURDAY

_____
_____
_____
_____

- ○ _____
- ○ _____
- ○ _____

18 SUNDAY

_____
_____
_____
_____
_____

- ○ _____
- ○ _____
- ○ _____

Notes and shit

_____
_____
_____

September 2022

Don't take any shit. Take breaks,

19 MONDAY | 20 TUESDAY | 21 WEDNESDAY

Important as fuck

Fucking grateful for...

walks and stuff you need. But don't take any shit.

22 THURSDAY	23 FRIDAY	24 SATURDAY

_____
_____
_____
_____
_____
_____
_____
_____
_____
_____
_____
○ _____
○ _____
○ _____

25 SUNDAY

_____
○ _____   ○ _____   _____
○ _____   ○ _____   _____
○ _____   ○ _____   _____
○ _____   ○ _____   _____
○ _____   ○ _____   _____
○ _____   ○ _____   _____
○ _____   ○ _____   ○ _____
○ _____   ○ _____   ○ _____
○ _____   ○ _____   ○ _____

Notes and *shit*

_____
_____
_____

September-October 2022

26 MONDAY	27 TUESDAY	28 WEDNESDAY

Important as *fuck*

Fucking grateful for...

You swear because you care

29 THURSDAY

_____
_____
_____
_____
_____
_____
_____
_____
_____
_____

○ _____
○ _____
○ _____
○ _____
○ _____
○ _____
○ _____
○ _____
○ _____

30 FRIDAY

_____
_____
_____
_____
_____
_____
_____
_____
_____
_____

○ _____
○ _____
○ _____
○ _____
○ _____
○ _____
○ _____
○ _____
○ _____

1 SATURDAY

○ _____
○ _____
○ _____

2 SUNDAY

_____
_____
_____
_____

○ _____
○ _____
○ _____

Notes and _shit_

_____
_____
_____

OCTOBER 2022

Sunday	Monday	Tuesday	Wednesday
2	3	4	5
9	10 Columbus Day (US) Thanksgiving (CA)	11	12
16	17	18	19
23	24	25	26
30	31 Halloween		

Keep fucking going

Thursday	Friday	Saturday
		1
6	7	8
13	14	15
20	21	22
27	28	29

Important shit

_____
_____
_____
_____
_____
_____
_____
_____
_____
_____
_____
_____
_____
_____
_____
_____
_____
_____
_____
_____
_____
_____
_____
_____
_____
_____

September

S	M	T	W	T	F	S
				1	2	3
4	5	6	7	8	9	10
11	12	13	14	15	16	17
18	19	20	21	22	23	24
25	26	27	28	29	30	

November

S	M	T	W	T	F	S
		1	2	3	4	5
6	7	8	9	10	11	12
13	14	15	16	17	18	19
20	21	22	23	24	25	26
27	28	29	30			

October 2022

3 MONDAY	4 TUESDAY	5 WEDNESDAY
_____	_____	_____
_____	_____	_____
_____	_____	_____
_____	_____	_____
_____	_____	_____
_____	_____	_____
_____	_____	_____
_____	_____	_____
_____	_____	_____
_____	_____	_____
_____	_____	_____
_____	_____	_____
_____	_____	_____
_____	_____	_____
○ _____	○ _____	○ _____
○ _____	○ _____	○ _____
○ _____	○ _____	○ _____
○ _____	○ _____	○ _____
○ _____	○ _____	○ _____
○ _____	○ _____	○ _____
○ _____	○ _____	○ _____
○ _____	○ _____	○ _____
○ _____	○ _____	○ _____

Important as *fuck*

Fucking grateful for...

If only closed minds came with closed fucking mouths

6 THURSDAY

_____
_____
_____
_____
_____
_____
_____
_____
_____
_____
_____
_____

- ○ _____
- ○ _____
- ○ _____
- ○ _____
- ○ _____
- ○ _____
- ○ _____
- ○ _____
- ○ _____

7 FRIDAY

_____
_____
_____
_____
_____
_____
_____
_____
_____

- ○ _____
- ○ _____
- ○ _____
- ○ _____
- ○ _____
- ○ _____
- ○ _____
- ○ _____
- ○ _____

8 SATURDAY

_____
_____
_____
_____

- ○ _____
- ○ _____
- ○ _____

9 SUNDAY

_____
_____
_____
_____
_____

- ○ _____
- ○ _____
- ○ _____

Notes and shit

_____
_____
_____

October 2022

There's a difference between talking shit

10 MONDAY
Columbus Day (US), Thanksgiving (CA)

11 TUESDAY

12 WEDNESDAY

_____

○
○
○
○
○
○
○
○
○

Important as fuck

_____
_____
_____

Fucking grateful for...

_____
_____
_____

about a person and talking truth about a shitty person

13 THURSDAY	14 FRIDAY	15 SATURDAY

_____

_____

_____

_____

_____

_____

_____ _____ _____

_____ _____ ○ _____

_____ _____ ○ _____

_____ _____ ○ _____

_____ _____

_____ _____ **16 SUNDAY**

_____ _____ _____

○ _____ ○ _____ _____

○ _____ ○ _____ _____

○ _____ ○ _____ _____

○ _____ ○ _____ _____

○ _____ ○ _____ _____

○ _____ ○ _____ _____

○ _____ ○ _____ ○ _____

○ _____ ○ _____ ○ _____

○ _____ ○ _____ ○ _____

Notes and *shit*

_____

_____

_____

October 2022

17 MONDAY	18 TUESDAY	19 WEDNESDAY
_____	_____	_____
_____	_____	_____
_____	_____	_____
_____	_____	_____
_____	_____	_____
_____	_____	_____
_____	_____	_____
_____	_____	_____
_____	_____	_____
_____	_____	_____
_____	_____	_____
_____	_____	_____
_____	_____	_____

- ◯ _____
- ◯ _____
- ◯ _____
- ◯ _____
- ◯ _____
- ◯ _____
- ◯ _____
- ◯ _____
- ◯ _____

Important as fuck

_____

_____

_____

Fucking grateful for...

_____

_____

_____

You are fucking amazing. —The Universe

20 THURSDAY

_____
_____
_____
_____
_____
_____
_____
_____
_____
_____
_____
_____

- ◯ _____
- ◯ _____
- ◯ _____
- ◯ _____
- ◯ _____
- ◯ _____
- ◯ _____
- ◯ _____
- ◯ _____

21 FRIDAY

_____
_____
_____
_____
_____
_____
_____
_____
_____

- ◯ _____
- ◯ _____
- ◯ _____
- ◯ _____
- ◯ _____
- ◯ _____
- ◯ _____
- ◯ _____
- ◯ _____

22 SATURDAY

_____
_____
_____
_____
- ◯ _____
- ◯ _____
- ◯ _____

23 SUNDAY

_____
_____
_____
_____
- ◯ _____
- ◯ _____
- ◯ _____

Notes and shit

_____
_____
_____

October 2022

24 MONDAY   25 TUESDAY   26 WEDNESDAY

Important as *fuck*

Fucking grateful for...

Show today who's the fucking boss

27 THURSDAY
28 FRIDAY
29 SATURDAY

_____
_____
_____
_____
_____
_____
_____
○ _____
○ _____
○ _____

30 SUNDAY

○ _____
○ _____
○ _____
○ _____
○ _____
○ _____
○ _____
○ _____
○ _____

○ _____
○ _____
○ _____

Notes and shit

_____
_____
_____

NOVEMBER 2022

Sunday	Monday	Tuesday	Wednesday
		1	2
6	7	8 Election Day (US)	9
13 Remembrance Sunday (UK)	14	15	16
20	21	22	23
27	28	29	30

Keep it classy as fuck

Thursday	Friday	Saturday
3	4	5
10	11 Veterans Day (US) Remembrance Day (CA, UK)	12
17	18	19
24	25 Thanksgiving Day (US)	26

Important shit

_____
_____
_____
_____
_____
_____
_____
_____
_____
_____
_____
_____
_____
_____
_____
_____
_____
_____
_____
_____
_____
_____
_____
_____
_____
_____

October

S	M	T	W	T	F	S
						1
2	3	4	5	6	7	8
9	10	11	12	13	14	15
16	17	18	19	20	21	22
23	24	25	26	27	28	29
30	31					

December

S	M	T	W	T	F	S
				1	2	3
4	5	6	7	8	9	10
11	12	13	14	15	16	17
18	19	20	21	22	23	24
25	26	27	28	29	30	31

October-November 2022

| 31 MONDAY | 1 TUESDAY | 2 WEDNESDAY |
| Halloween | | |

_____
_____
_____
_____
_____
_____
_____
_____
_____
_____
_____
_____

○ _____
○ _____
○ _____
○ _____
○ _____
○ _____
○ _____
○ _____
○ _____

Important as *fuck*

_____
_____
_____

Fucking grateful for...

_____
_____
_____

When life gives you lemons, throw them at assholes

3 THURSDAY

_____
_____
_____
_____
_____
_____
_____
_____
_____
_____
_____

- ○ _____
- ○ _____
- ○ _____
- ○ _____
- ○ _____
- ○ _____
- ○ _____
- ○ _____
- ○ _____

4 FRIDAY

_____
_____
_____
_____
_____
_____
_____
_____

- ○ _____
- ○ _____
- ○ _____
- ○ _____
- ○ _____
- ○ _____
- ○ _____
- ○ _____
- ○ _____

5 SATURDAY

_____
_____
_____
_____
- ○ _____
- ○ _____
- ○ _____

6 SUNDAY

_____
_____
_____
_____
- ○ _____
- ○ _____
- ○ _____

Notes and shit

_____
_____
_____

November 2022

7 MONDAY	8 TUESDAY Election Day (US)	9 WEDNESDAY
_____	_____	_____
_____	_____	_____
_____	_____	_____
_____	_____	_____
_____	_____	_____
_____	_____	_____
_____	_____	_____
_____	_____	_____
_____	_____	_____
_____	_____	_____
_____	_____	_____
_____	_____	_____
_____	_____	_____
_____	_____	_____

○ _____ ○ _____ ○ _____
○ _____ ○ _____ ○ _____
○ _____ ○ _____ ○ _____
○ _____ ○ _____ ○ _____
○ _____ ○ _____ ○ _____
○ _____ ○ _____ ○ _____
○ _____ ○ _____ ○ _____
○ _____ ○ _____ ○ _____
○ _____ ○ _____ ○ _____

Important as *fuck*

_____
_____
_____

Fucking grateful for...

_____
_____
_____

You can't make everyone fucking happy. You're not a taco.

10 THURSDAY

11 FRIDAY
Veterans Day (US), Remembrance Day (CA, UK)

12 SATURDAY

- ○
- ○
- ○

13 SUNDAY
Remembrance Sunday (UK)

Thursday checklist:
- ○
- ○
- ○
- ○
- ○
- ○
- ○
- ○
- ○

Friday checklist:
- ○
- ○
- ○
- ○
- ○
- ○
- ○
- ○
- ○

Sunday checklist:
- ○
- ○
- ○

Notes and shit

November 2022

14 MONDAY

15 TUESDAY

16 WEDNESDAY

_____
_____
_____
_____
_____
_____
_____
_____
_____
_____
_____

○ _____
○ _____
○ _____
○ _____
○ _____
○ _____
○ _____
○ _____
○ _____

Important as *fuck*

_____
_____
_____

Fucking grateful for...

_____
_____
_____

Or torture them with sarcasm. You have options.

17 THURSDAY

_____
_____
_____
_____
_____
_____
_____
_____
_____
_____
○ _____
○ _____
○ _____
○ _____
○ _____
○ _____
○ _____
○ _____
○ _____

18 FRIDAY

_____
_____
_____
_____
_____
_____
_____
_____
_____
_____
○ _____
○ _____
○ _____
○ _____
○ _____
○ _____
○ _____
○ _____
○ _____

19 SATURDAY

_____
_____
_____
_____
_____
○ _____
○ _____
○ _____

20 SUNDAY

_____
_____
_____
_____
_____
_____
○ _____
○ _____
○ _____

Notes and shit

_____
_____
_____

November 2022

Important as *fuck*

Fucking grateful for...

Let your dreams be your fucking wings

24 THURSDAY
Thanksgiving Day (US)

_____
_____
_____
_____
_____
_____
_____
_____
_____
_____

- ◯ _____
- ◯ _____
- ◯ _____
- ◯ _____
- ◯ _____
- ◯ _____
- ◯ _____
- ◯ _____
- ◯ _____

25 FRIDAY

_____
_____
_____
_____
_____
_____
_____

- ◯ _____
- ◯ _____
- ◯ _____
- ◯ _____
- ◯ _____
- ◯ _____
- ◯ _____
- ◯ _____
- ◯ _____

26 SATURDAY

_____
_____
_____
- ◯ _____
- ◯ _____
- ◯ _____

27 SUNDAY

_____
_____
_____
_____
- ◯ _____
- ◯ _____
- ◯ _____

Notes and shit

_____
_____
_____

DECEMBER 2022

Sunday	Monday	Tuesday	Wednesday
November S M T W T F S 1 2 3 4 5 6 7 8 9 10 11 12 13 14 15 16 17 18 19 20 21 22 23 24 25 26 27 28 29 30	**January 2023** S M T W T F S 1 2 3 4 5 6 7 8 9 10 11 12 13 14 15 16 17 18 19 20 21 22 23 24 25 26 27 28 29 30 31		
4	5	6	7
11	12	13	14
18 Hanukkah, begins at sundown	19	20	21
25 Christmas Day	26 Boxing Day (CA, UK) Kwanzaa begins (US)	27 Bank Holiday (UK)	28

Finish on a fucking high note

Thursday	Friday	Saturday
1	2	3
8	9	10
15	16	17
22	23	24
29	30	31

Important shit

_____
_____
_____
_____
_____
_____
_____
_____
_____
_____
_____
_____
_____
_____
_____
_____
_____
_____
_____
_____
_____
_____
_____
_____
_____
_____
_____

November-December 2022

28 MONDAY	29 TUESDAY	30 WEDNESDAY

_____

Important as _fuck_

_____

$\mathcal{F}$**ucking** grateful for...

_____

You are a fucking rock star

1 THURSDAY

_____

_____

_____

_____

_____

_____

_____

_____

_____

_____

_____

- ◯ _____
- ◯ _____
- ◯ _____
- ◯ _____
- ◯ _____
- ◯ _____
- ◯ _____
- ◯ _____
- ◯ _____

2 FRIDAY

_____

_____

_____

_____

_____

_____

_____

_____

_____

_____

- ◯ _____
- ◯ _____
- ◯ _____
- ◯ _____
- ◯ _____
- ◯ _____
- ◯ _____
- ◯ _____
- ◯ _____

3 SATURDAY

_____

_____

_____

_____

- ◯ _____
- ◯ _____
- ◯ _____

4 SUNDAY

_____

_____

_____

_____

_____

- ◯ _____
- ◯ _____
- ◯ _____

Notes and shit

_____

_____

_____

December 2022

5 MONDAY	6 TUESDAY	7 WEDNESDAY
_____	_____	_____
_____	_____	_____
_____	_____	_____
_____	_____	_____
_____	_____	_____
_____	_____	_____
_____	_____	_____
_____	_____	_____
_____	_____	_____
_____	_____	_____
_____	_____	_____
○ _____	○ _____	○ _____
○ _____	○ _____	○ _____
○ _____	○ _____	○ _____
○ _____	○ _____	○ _____
○ _____	○ _____	○ _____
○ _____	○ _____	○ _____
○ _____	○ _____	○ _____
○ _____	○ _____	○ _____
○ _____	○ _____	○ _____

Important as *fuck*

_____

_____

_____

Fucking grateful for...

_____

_____

_____

If only swearing burned calories

8 THURSDAY

_____
_____
_____
_____
_____
_____
_____
_____
_____
_____
_____
_____

- ◯ _____
- ◯ _____
- ◯ _____
- ◯ _____
- ◯ _____
- ◯ _____
- ◯ _____
- ◯ _____
- ◯ _____

9 FRIDAY

_____
_____
_____
_____
_____
_____
_____
_____
_____
_____
_____

- ◯ _____
- ◯ _____
- ◯ _____
- ◯ _____
- ◯ _____
- ◯ _____
- ◯ _____
- ◯ _____
- ◯ _____

10 SATURDAY

_____
_____
_____
_____

- ◯ _____
- ◯ _____
- ◯ _____

11 SUNDAY

_____
_____
_____
_____
_____

- ◯ _____
- ◯ _____
- ◯ _____

Notes and shit

_____
_____
_____

December 2022

12 MONDAY	13 TUESDAY	14 WEDNESDAY
_____	_____	_____
_____	_____	_____
_____	_____	_____
_____	_____	_____
_____	_____	_____
_____	_____	_____
_____	_____	_____
_____	_____	_____
_____	_____	_____
_____	_____	_____
_____	_____	_____
_____	_____	_____
○ _____	○ _____	○ _____
○ _____	○ _____	○ _____
○ _____	○ _____	○ _____
○ _____	○ _____	○ _____
○ _____	○ _____	○ _____
○ _____	○ _____	○ _____
○ _____	○ _____	○ _____
○ _____	○ _____	○ _____
○ _____	○ _____	○ _____

Important as *fuck*

Fucking grateful for...

Smile a lot. The assholes hate that.

15 THURSDAY

_____
_____
_____
_____
_____
_____
_____
_____
_____
_____
_____

- ◯ _____
- ◯ _____
- ◯ _____
- ◯ _____
- ◯ _____
- ◯ _____
- ◯ _____
- ◯ _____
- ◯ _____

16 FRIDAY

_____
_____
_____
_____
_____
_____
_____

- ◯ _____
- ◯ _____
- ◯ _____
- ◯ _____
- ◯ _____
- ◯ _____
- ◯ _____
- ◯ _____
- ◯ _____

17 SATURDAY

_____
_____
_____

- ◯ _____
- ◯ _____
- ◯ _____

18 SUNDAY
Hanukkah, begins at sundown

_____
_____
_____
_____
_____

- ◯ _____
- ◯ _____
- ◯ _____

Notes and shit

_____
_____
_____

December 2022

19 MONDAY	20 TUESDAY	21 WEDNESDAY

Important as *fuck*

Fucking grateful for...

Way to keep it fucking real

22 THURSDAY

_____
_____
_____
_____
_____
_____
_____
_____
_____
_____
_____
_____

○ _____
○ _____
○ _____
○ _____
○ _____
○ _____
○ _____
○ _____
○ _____

23 FRIDAY

_____
_____
_____
_____
_____
_____
_____
_____
_____
_____
_____

○ _____
○ _____
○ _____
○ _____
○ _____
○ _____
○ _____
○ _____
○ _____

24 SATURDAY

_____
_____
_____
_____
_____
○ _____
○ _____
○ _____

25 SUNDAY
Christmas Day

_____
_____
_____
_____
_____
○ _____
○ _____
○ _____

Notes and shit

_____
_____
_____

December 2022-January 2023

26 MONDAY
Boxing Day (CA, UK)

27 TUESDAY
Bank Holiday (UK)

28 WEDNESDAY

Important as *fuck*

Fucking grateful for...

You are amazing as fuck. Keep that shit up.

29 THURSDAY	30 FRIDAY	31 SATURDAY

_____ _____ _____
_____ _____ _____
_____ _____ _____
_____ _____ _____
_____ _____ _____
_____ _____ _____
_____ _____ ○ _____
_____ _____ ○ _____
_____ _____ ○ _____

1 SUNDAY
New Year's Day

○ _____ ○ _____ _____
○ _____ ○ _____ _____
○ _____ ○ _____ _____
○ _____ ○ _____ _____
○ _____ ○ _____ _____
○ _____ ○ _____ ○ _____
○ _____ ○ _____ ○ _____
○ _____ ○ _____ ○ _____
○ _____ ○ _____

Notes and shit

_____
_____
_____

My Brilliant Thoughts & Shit

My Brilliant Thoughts & Shit

_____

_____

_____

_____

_____

_____

_____

_____

_____

_____

_____

_____

_____

_____

_____

_____

_____

_____

_____

_____

_____

_____

_____

My Brilliant Thoughts & Shit

My Brilliant Thoughts & Shit

My Brilliant Thoughts & Shit

My Brilliant Thoughts & Shit

My Brilliant Thoughts & Shit

My Brilliant Thoughts & Shit

_____

_____

_____

_____

_____

_____

_____

_____

_____

_____

_____

_____

_____

_____

_____

_____

_____

_____

_____

_____

_____

Thank you for trying us out!

One last reminder:

You are amazing and deserve to be happy as fuck!

Have comments or questions about our books? Want freebies to brighten your day?

Please email us at
sassyquotespress@gmail.com

For more sarcastic planners, journals and coloring books, please visit

https://www.amazon.com/~/e/B08TGS2ZBL

Favor please :)

Would you take a quick minute to leave us a rating/review on Amazon? It makes a HUGE difference and we would really appreciate it.

THANK YOU!

Printed in Great Britain
by Amazon

72285943R00086